AMAZING ANIMALS

PLATYPUSES

BY ASHLEY GISH

CREATIVE EDUCATION • CREATIVE PAPERBACKS

Published by Creative Education
and Creative Paperbacks
P.O. Box 227, Mankato, Minnesota 56002
Creative Education and Creative Paperbacks
are imprints of The Creative Company
www.thecreativecompany.us

Design by The Design Lab
Production by Blue Design
Art direction by Graham Morgan

Images by Getty Images/Jason Edwards, 14, John Carnemolla, 6, Martin Harvey, 18, The Sydney Morning Herald, 5; Shutterstock/John Carnemolla, 13, Matis75, cover, 1; Unsplash/Birmingham Museums Trust, 8, Michael Jerrard, 21, Ronald Bradford, 2, Trevor McKinnon, 9; Wikimedia Commons/Charles J. Sharp, 10, 17, Dakota Brown, 2, 3, 4, 6, 7, 8, 10, 11, 12, 13, 14, 15, 16, 18, 19, 20, 21, 22, 24, E.Lonnon., 20, Garst, Warren, 11, John Gould, 23, Matteo De Stefano/MUSE, 16, Wairambar Rainforest, 7

Cataloging-in-Publication data is available from
the Library of Congress.
Library Binding ISBN: 9798895810583
Paperback ISBN: 9798896800118
eBook ISBN: 9798895811849
LCCN: 2025011356

Printed in China

Table of Contents

What animal has fur and a flat tail like a beaver, but lays eggs and has a bill like a duck? A platypus, of course! Some people call these animals "duck-billed platypuses." Their soft bill feels like a wet pencil eraser.

In the past, people thought platypuses were fake animals that didn't really exist.

Platypuses use their flat tail to steer while swimming.

Platypuses are excellent swimmers. They keep their eyes, ears, and nostrils closed when swimming. They find their way using **sensors** in their bill.

sensor something that feels changes in the surrounding area

Platypus fur is dark brown on top and light brown on the belly. It stays dry even in the water. Adult platypuses are about the size of a house cat. They use their strong front legs for both swimming and digging.

Platypuses swish their head from side to side as they swim. This helps them sense prey in the water.

Platypuses do not have teeth. They grind up their food using horny plates inside their bill.

Platypuses live in eastern Australia and Tasmania. They live near creeks, slow rivers, and lakes. They dig **burrows** at the water's edge. Platypuses rest during the day. They come out early in the morning and at night to find food in the water.

burrow a hole in the ground where some animals live

When small animals move in the water, platypuses can feel them.

Platypuses eat mostly insect larvae, water bugs, tadpoles, and shrimp. They sometimes eat snails and worms. Platypuses hunt underwater for up to two minutes at a time. They collect food in their cheek pouches to carry to the surface.

larva the young, wingless, wormlike form of many insects

Young platypuses are often called puggles.

Platypuses are one of two kinds of **mammals** that lays eggs. The mother platypus makes a nest in her burrow for her eggs. Baby platypuses hatch from the eggs. They drink milk from their mother. The milk drips from two patches under her fur.

mammal an animal that is warm-blooded and feeds its babies milk

Platypuses may share the same body of water. But they do not eat, sleep, or swim in groups. Puggles live with their mother for about four months. Then they leave the nest to live on their own.

Platypuses can live for up to 20 years.

Platypuses may eat up to half their body weight in prey every night.

Platypus fur glows blue-green in ultraviolet light. Humans can't see this without special lamps. No one knows for sure why platypus fur glows.

ultraviolet a kind of light beyond violet that some animals can see

The platypus is one of only a few **venomous** mammals. The male has sharp spurs on his heels. To protect himself from harm, he can stab a **predator** with the spurs. This can feel worse than hundreds of hornet stings.

predator an animal that hunts other animals for food

venomous using teeth, stingers, or spurs to deliver poison

A Platypus Tale

The land,

water, and sky animals each claimed to be the most special. Land animals had fur, water animals could swim, and birds laid eggs. Each group invited Platypus to join, but she refused. She knew many things made her special without needing to belong to any group.

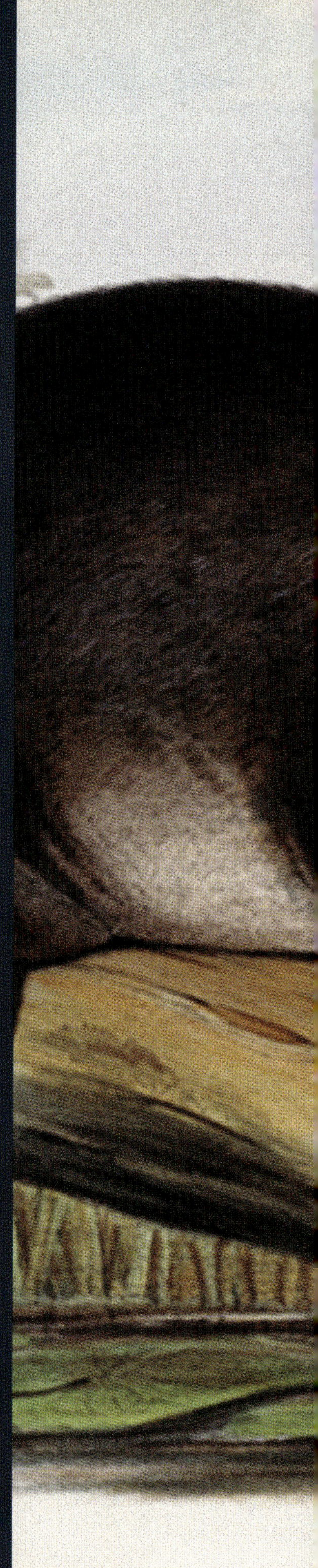

Read More

Mallory, Louis. Electric Animals: *Platypuses Sense Electricity!* New York: Gareth Stevens, 2024.

Olson, Elsie. *Platypuses*. Minneapolis: Abdo Publishing, 2025.

Sexton, Colleen. *Platypus*. Minneapolis: Bearport Publishing, 2021.

Websites

Duck-Billed Platypus
https://kids.nationalgeographic.com/animals/mammals/facts/platypus
Learn more about the duck-billed platypus on National Geographic Kids.

Platypus: The Duck-Billed Mammal
https://sdzwildlifeexplorers.org/animals/platypus
Read more and see pictures of platypuses on the San Diego Zoo Wildlife Explorers site.

Index